Pebble® Plus

Weather Basics

Clouds

by Erin Edison

Consulting Editor: Gail Saunders-Smith, PhD

CAPSTONE PRESS
a capstone imprint

Pebble Plus is published by Capstone Press,
151 Good Counsel Drive, P.O. Box 669, Mankato, Minnesota 56002.
www.capstonepub.com

 Books published by Capstone Press are manufactured with paper
containing at least 10 percent post-consumer waste.

Library of Congress Cataloging-in-Publication Data
Edison, Erin.
  Clouds / by Erin Edison.
      p. cm.—(Pebble plus. Weather basics)
  Summary: "Simple text and full-color photographs describe how clouds form and the different types of clouds"—
Provided by publisher.
  Includes bibliographical references and index.
  ISBN 978-1-4296-6057-0 (library binding)
  ISBN 978-1-4296-7077-7 (paperback)
  1. Clouds—Juvenile literature. 2. Clouds—Diurnal variations—Juvenile literature. I. Title. II. Series.
  QC921.35.E35 2012
  551.57'6—dc22   2010053936

Editorial Credits
Erika L. Shores, editor; Kyle Grenz, designer; Laura Manthe, production specialist

Photo Credits
Dreamstime: Robert Adrian Hillman, 11; Getty Images Inc.: The Image Bank/Tyler Stableford, 21; Shutterstock:
2happy, back cover, andreiuc88, 19, Christophe Testi, 17, Dudarev Mikhail, 9, Gulei Ivan, cover, Nataliia Melnychuk, 5,
TobagoCays, 15, tonobalaguerf, 13, vovan, 1, Yuriy Kulyk, 7

Artistic Effects
Shutterstock: marcus55

**Capstone Press thanks Mike Shores, earth science teacher at RBA Public Charter School in Mankato,
      Minnesota, for his assistance on this book.**

Note to Parents and Teachers

The Weather Basics series supports national science standards related to earth science. This
book describes and illustrates clouds. The images support early readers in understanding the
text. The repetition of words and phrases helps early readers learn new words. This book
also introduces early readers to subject-specific vocabulary words, which are defined in the
Glossary section. Early readers may need assistance to read some words and to use the Table of
Contents, Glossary, Read More, Internet Sites, and Index sections of the book.

Printed in the United States of America in North Mankato, Minnesota.

032011   006110CGF11

Table of Contents

What Are Clouds?

Clouds move across the sky.

Clouds can be all shapes and sizes.

Some clouds are big and puffy.

Others are thin and wispy.

Clouds form when warm air
rises and cools.
Tiny water droplets stick
to dust and other particles
in the air to make clouds.

Clouds drop precipitation on land.

Snow falls when the air is

32 degrees Fahrenheit

(0 degrees Celsius) or lower.

Rain falls when it's warmer.

Types of Clouds

Scientists study cloud shapes.

The shapes tell what kind

of weather is coming.

Cirrus clouds are high and thin.

They mean good weather.

Cumulus clouds have
flat bottoms and puffy tops.
Small, white cumulus clouds
mean we'll have good weather.

Cumulonimbus clouds mean
bad weather is coming.
These tall, puffy clouds bring
thunderstorms, hail,
and even tornadoes.

Gray, flat stratus clouds

cover most of the sky.

They form low in the sky.

Snow or rain sometimes falls

from stratus clouds.

Fog is a cloud too. Fog happens
when a cloud forms near
the ground. Fog goes away
when wind and heat
evaporate the water.

Wind Moves Clouds

Clouds carry rain and snow. Wind pushes clouds across the sky. Clouds bring water to places all over the world.

Glossary

droplet—a small drop of liquid

evaporate—the action of a liquid changing into a gas; heat causes water to evaporate

hail—balls of ice that form in clouds and fall to the ground

particle—a tiny piece of something; water droplets stick to dust, salt, and other tiny particles in the air to form clouds

precipitation—water that falls from clouds to the earth's surface; precipitation can be rain, hail, sleet, or snow

tornado—a large, twisting cloud that produces high winds; tornadoes form over land

Read More

Flanagan, Alice K. *Rain.* Weather Watch. Mankato, Minn.: Child's World, Inc., 2010.

Goldsmith, Mike. *The Weather.* Now We Know About. New York: Crabtree Pub., 2010.

Sterling, Kristin. *It's Cloudy Today.* What's the Weather Like? Minneapolis: Lerner Publications Co., 2010.

Internet Sites

FactHound offers a safe, fun way to find Internet sites related to this book. All of the sites on FactHound have been researched by our staff.

Here's all you do:

Visit *www.facthound.com*

Type in this code: 9781429660570

Check out projects, games and lots more at
www.capstonekids.com

Index

Word Count: 194
Grade: 1
Early-Intervention Level: 19